VOLCANOES
AND EARTHQUAKES

Discover Earth's amazing places

Susie Brooks

Published in paperback in 2016 by Wayland
Copyright © Wayland 2016

Editor: Elizabeth Brent
Designer: Rocket Design (East Anglia) Ltd

Dewey number: 551.2-dc23

ISBN   978 0 7502 9075 3
eBook ISBN   978 0 7502 9074 6

Printed in China

10 9 8 7 6 5 4 3 2 1

MIX
Paper from
responsible sources
FSC® C104740

Pictures by Shutterstock except: Cover: Michele Falzone/JAI/Corbis; pp4–5: Stefan Chabluk; p4 (top): Joe Carini/Getty Images, (bottom): CHEN WS/Shutterstock.com; p5 (bottom): Stefan Chabluk; p6 (left): James P. Blair/Getty Images, (bottom): Stefan Chabluk; p7 (left): Stefan Chabluk, (right): fpolat69/Shutterstock.com; p9 (top): Stefan Chabluk; p11 (middle): Tom Pfeiffer/Volcano Discovery; pp12–13: Stefan Chabluk; p14: JIJI PRESS/AFP/Getty Images; p15 (top): Stefan Chabluk, (bottom left): TEPCO/Xinhua Press/Corbis, (bottom right): Prometheus72/Shutterstock.com; p16 (bottom): Stefan Chabluk; p17 (top): DeAgostini/Getty Images; p19 (bottom left): Stefan Chabluk; p21 (top right): Stefan Chabluk; p22 (bottom left): Lilja Kristjansdo/NordicPhotos/Getty Images; p23 (top left): Stefan Chabluk; (top right): Philippe Bourseiller/Getty Images, (bottom left): Pool AVENTURIER/LOVINY/Gamma-Rapho via Getty Images; p25 (top left): Stefan Chabluk; p26 (bottom left): NigelSpiers/Shutterstock.com; p27 (top left): Ralph White/CORBIS, (bottom left): Travel Ink/Getty Images, (bottom right): Arctic-Images/Getty Images; p28 (top right): Carsten Peter/National Geographic Creative/Corbis, (bottom left): Carsten Peter/National Geographic Creative/Corbis, (bottom right): Tim Clayton/101010/Corbis; p29 (top middle): f8grapher/Shutterstock.com, (top right): Stefan Chabluk, (bottom left): YUYA SHINO/Reuters/Corbis

The website addresses (URLs) included in this book were valid at the time of going to press. However, it is possible that contents or addresses may have changed since the publication of this book. No responsibility for any such changes can be accepted by either the author or the Publisher.

Wayland, an imprint of Hachette Children's Group
Part of Hodder & Stoughton
Carmelite House
50 Victoria Embankment
London
EC4Y 0DZ

An Hachette UK Company
www.hachette.co.uk
www.hachettechildrens.co.uk

CONTENTS

Where on Earth are volcanoes & earthquakes?

GIANT VOLCANO

The biggest active volcano is Hawaii's Mauna Loa, towering 4,170m above sea level. From its base on the seafloor to its peak, it's taller than Mount Everest!

TRAVEL CHAOS!

In 2010, ash from a volcano in Iceland disrupted air travel across Europe for six days – 100,000 flights were cancelled!

POP-UP ISLANDS

Thousands of volcanoes erupt deep under the sea. Sometimes they build up to form new islands – that's how places like Hawaii and Iceland began.

The land we walk on might seem super-solid, but compared to the rest of Earth it's pretty thin! The surface of our planet is made up of huge slabs of rock called plates, which float on hot rock beneath. Most volcanoes and earthquakes happen where these plates meet.

Volcanoes and earthquakes affect people's lives in many different parts of the globe. In this book you'll discover WHERE, HOW and WHY ON EARTH these powerhouses rock our world.

- Volcanoes
- Earthquakes
- Plate boundaries

FERTILE

Volcanic soil is rich and popular with farmers.

CONSTANT ACTIVITY

There's a 100% chance of an earthquake happening today — even while you're reading this page! They occur about twice a minute.

QUAKES

* 1,000,000+ earthquakes happen every year
* 500,000 of these are detectable
* 100,000 can be felt
* 100 cause damage.

LAND ERUPTIONS

* 1,500 land volcanoes are active
* 550 different volcanoes have erupted since records began
* 50–70 of these erupt each year
* 20 could be erupting now!

DEVASTATION

In 2015, a deadly earthquake struck Nepal, killing more than 8,000 people.

SUPER SHAKER

The longest recorded earthquake lasted 8–10 minutes and caused the 2004 Indian Ocean tsunami (see page 13). Most earthquakes last a minute or less.

NON-STOP

Japan records more than 1,500 earthquakes a year (most are too mild to cause damage).

EAST AFRICAN RIFT

Lots of volcanoes and earthquakes occur along the East African Rift – a tear in the African plate.

CRUST - solid rock

MANTLE - molten rock

OUTER CORE - liquid metal

INNER CORE - solid metal

LAYERS

Relative to its size, Earth's crust is thinner than an apple skin.

What shocks an earthquake into action?

Earth's plates are constantly moving and jostling. They do this no faster than your hair grows, shifting by just a few centimetres each year. Where they press against each other, they put the rock under great strain. Eventually the rock slips, causing an earthquake.

San Andreas is a strike-slip fault.

Plates come together in different ways. If they meet head-on, they can push each other upwards and form mountains. Some plates grind sideways, and others dive one below the other or pull apart. The cracks they leave in the Earth's crust are known as faults.

Not all faults are visible on the surface, but the San Andreas fault looks like a giant scar across California, USA. Movement along it means that the cities of San Francisco and Los Angeles are creeping closer together – in 12 million years they could be side by side!

FAULT TYPES

normal fault

reverse fault

strike-slip fault

25221. Neg 34455

THE SAN ANDREAS FAULT IS ABOUT 1,300KM LONG AND MORE THAN 20 MILLION YEARS OLD!

~ SHOCKING! ~

When the rocks along a fault suddenly slip, energy blasts out in the form of shock waves.

The spot underground where the rocks first give way is called the focus.

The epicentre is directly above the focus, on the surface. It's the place that usually shakes the most.

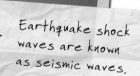

Earthquake shock waves are known as seismic waves.

AFTERSHOCK

Often rocks continue to tremble for hours or days after a big earthquake, causing smaller tremors called aftershocks.

ROCKING

* Seismic waves can travel for thousands of kilometres. Some whizz through Earth at 8km per second – that's like running 10 full marathons in a minute!

* Seismic waves that travel along Earth's surface are known as surface waves. They are slower than deep seismic waves, but cause more damage.

* Deep earthquakes create much weaker surface waves than shallower earthquakes.

* Some surface waves jerk the ground from side to side, while others shake it up and down.

Most earthquakes strike less than 80km below Earth's surface.

What makes a volcano erupt?

It's scorchingly hot inside Earth – so hot that the rock melts! This molten rock, called magma, is full of bubbles of gas, so it's lighter than the solid rock above it. The magma rises and pushes at the surface rock... until it finds an opportunity to burst out.

Think of a shaken-up can of fizzy drink. The bubbles of gas are compressed inside, but when they have a chance to escape, they explode all over the place! It's the same with magma. When it finds a weakness in Earth's crust, it bursts through and forms a volcano.

THE TEMPERATURE IN EARTH'S CORE IS AROUND 6,000°C – AS HOT AS THE SUN'S SURFACE!

Some volcanoes happen where plates pull apart, and magma rises into the gap. Others erupt when one plate sinks and melts beneath another. A hot spot is where a stream of rising magma scalds a hole in the middle of a plate.

HUBBLE BUBBLE

1. Over time, pressure in a magma chamber builds.
2. The magma bubbles up through a pipe, or conduit.
3. Magma bursts out through the vent.

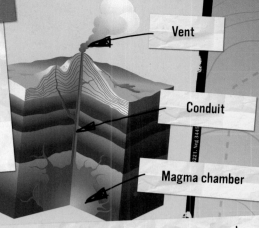

Vent

Conduit

Magma chamber

Magma chambers can lurk quietly underground for hundreds of years before an eruption.

THERE SHE BLOWS!

LIFE OF A VOLCANO

Because the plates are constantly shifting, magma has to find new places to get to the surface.

This means new volcanoes can appear - and some old volcanoes become:

EXTINCT

(when scientists don't expect them ever to erupt again)

or

DORMANT

(when they're not active now but could one day erupt again).

An **ACTIVE** volcano is one that has erupted at least once in the last 10,000 years.

Edinburgh Castle in Scotland is built on an extinct volcano!

When a plate keeps moving over a hot spot, a chain of volcanoes can appear. The Hawaiian islands are an example of this.

DANGER!

Some volcanoes erupt unexpectedly when they're thought to be extinct. This happened with Mount Vesuvius in 79CE.

Could you escape an erupting volcano?

You hear a hiss, the ground shakes... then BOOM! The top of a nearby mountain turns to fire. Burning hot rock, ash and gases erupt out of the Earth and either pour down slopes in sizzling rivers or explode high into the sky. What are your chances of escape?

When magma reaches the surface, it's known as lava. This is the red-hot rock you see creeping down the sides of a volcano. Most lava flows slowly — you could outrun it. But when it forms a channel, it can move much faster.

• A lava flow burns or buries everything in its path, including roads and buildings.

• Sometimes lava can jet upwards like a fountain, or shoot out in lumps called 'volcanic bombs'.

LAVA CAN BE AS HOT AS 1,200°C – THAT'S FOUR TIMES YOUR OVEN'S MAXIMUM TEMPERATURE!

DEADLY ERUPTIONS!

>> EXPLOSION <<

Some eruptions are explosive. They blast splintered rock, lava, ash and gas kilometres into the air.

>> VOLCANIC ASH <<

is hot and heavy. It can darken skies, coat cities and collapse roofs.

A PYROCLASTIC FLOW

is a deadly avalanche of scorching ash, gas and rock. It thunders downhill at 100-300kph – you've no chance if you're in its path.

In 79CE, people were trapped and killed by pyroclastic flows from Mount Vesuvius, Italy. You can still see casts of their bodies, made from hollows in the ash.

MUD FLOW

When ash mixes with water, such as snowmelt or heavy rain, a mudflow called a lahar can form. Large lahars, hundreds of metres wide and tens of metres deep, can race along at more than twice the top speed of sprinter Usain Bolt.

STEER CLEAR!

The answer is, it's best to steer clear of active volcanoes! If you do find yourself near one, learn the local safety advice (see page 28).

Where was the world's worst earthquake?

Alaska, USA, 1964
(magnitude 9.2): 131 died

San Francisco, USA, 1906
(magnitude 7.9): 700 died

☠ **DEADLIEST RECENT**

>> Haiti, 2010 <<
(magnitude 7)

The death toll was 230,000 (or up to 316,000 according to some figures). This was a shallow earthquake in a densely populated, poorly built area.

Scientists can measure the strength, or magnitude, of an earthquake. But the strongest quakes aren't necessarily the deadliest. It usually depends on how close they happen to big communities, or to the sea, where giant waves called tsunamis can charge far and wide.

☠ **STRONGEST ON RECORD**

>> Chile, 1960 <<
(magnitude 9.5)

About 2,000 people died – most from a tsunami that also raced across the Pacific Ocean, causing deaths as far away as Hawaii, Japan and the Philippines.

SCIENTISTS USE AN INSTRUMENT CALLED A SEISMOMETER TO MEASURE SHOCK WAVES FROM AN EARTHQUAKE.

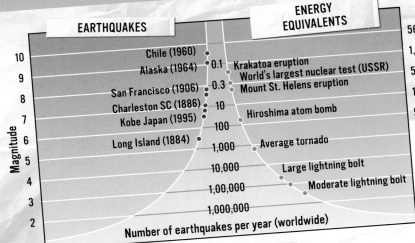

EARTHQUAKES

ENERGY EQUIVALENTS

Magnitude		Number per year	Energy Equivalents	Energy release (equivalent: kilograms of explosive)

Magnitude scale (left axis): 10, 9, 8, 7, 6, 5, 4, 3, 2

- Chile (1960) — 10
- Alaska (1964) — 9 — 0.1 — Krakatoa eruption / World's largest nuclear test (USSR) — 56,000,000,000,000 / 1,800,000,000,000
- San Francisco (1906) — 0.3 — Mount St. Helens eruption — 56,000,000,000
- Charleston SC (1886) — 8 — 10 — 18,000,000,000
- Kobe Japan (1995) — 7 — 100 — Hiroshima atom bomb — 56,000,000
- Long Island (1884) — 6 — 1,000 — Average tornado — 1,800,000
- 5 — 10,000 — 56,000
- 4 — 1,00,000 — Large lightning bolt — 1800
- 3 — 1,000,000 — Moderate lightning bolt — 56
- 2

Number of earthquakes per year (worldwide)

Energy release (equivalent: kilograms of explosive)

THE MOMENT MAGNITUDE SCALE

Scientists use an instrument called a seismometer to measure shock waves from an earthquake.

They rate its strength on the moment magnitude scale. Each magnitude is 33 times stronger than the last – so a magnitude 9 is 35,937 (33 x 33 x 33) times stronger than a 6!

Honshu, Japan, 2011
(mag 9): 16,000 died
(see pp14/15)

Sichuan, China, 2008
(mag 7.9): nearly 90,000 died

Bam, Iran, 2003
(mag 6.6): 31,000 died

 DEADLIEST ON RECORD

>> Shaanxi, China, 1556 <<
(magnitude unknown)

About 830,000 people died – enough to fill Wembley Stadium nine times over. Most victims were living in Yaodongs, or 'house caves', which collapsed with the cliffs that they were built into.

☠ **DEADLIEST TSUNAMI**

>> Indian Ocean, 2004 <<
(magnitude 9)

Waves travelled for 2,000km at up to 800kph, damaging 14 countries and killing 23,000 people.

Walls of water up to 10m high hit the coastline of Sumatra, Indonesia, near the epicentre.

Which earthquake caused a nuclear disaster?

In 2011, a magnitude 9 earthquake struck off the coast of Japan and triggered a deadly tsunami. As well as killing nearly 16,000 people and leaving hundreds of thousands homeless, it damaged the Fukushima nuclear power plant and caused a radioactive leak.

The earthquake struck where one plate dives below another. It was the world's fifth most powerful earthquake and the strongest in Japan since records began. Hundreds of aftershocks (many of magnitude 6 or more) followed in the weeks after the main quake.

Japan is well prepared for earthquakes, but it underestimated this one. Less than half an hour after the quake, the first of many tsunami waves hit the coastline. They overtopped protective seawalls and destroyed three-storey buildings, travelling as far as 10km inland.

THE QUAKE WAS STRONG ENOUGH TO SPIN EARTH A FRACTION FASTER, AND SHORTEN OUR DAY BY ABOUT A MILLIONTH OF A SECOND!

The tsunami flooded an area bigger than 78,000 football pitches.

HOW A TSUNAMI FORMS

epicentre

During a quake the sea floor either rises or sinks, displacing a large amount of water.

Waves move away at high speeds. In deep water, tsunamis can be as small as 60cm high, but travel at more than 700kph.

The waves slow down but grow bigger as they reach shallower water near the coast.

The tsunami hits the coast, devastating all in its path.

MELTDOWN

The tsunami damaged the cooling system at Fukushima Daiichi Nuclear Power Plant, causing a major meltdown.

Around 300,000 people were evacuated from the area due to dangerous radioactive leaks.

Three years later, contaminated water from the plant was still leaking into the ocean.

EARTHQUAKE HAZARDS

Strong earthquakes can cause damage and death in many ways, including:

- ☠ Collapse or rupturing of buildings, bridges and roads
- ☠ Fires, often started by torn power lines
- ☠ Landslides or avalanches
- ☠ Flooding from broken dams or levees
- ☠ Tsunamis

Why are volcanoes different shapes?

Not all volcanoes look like a perfect cone. Some sprawl outwards like an upturned bowl; others blow their tops off when they erupt. A volcano can start small and grow enormous – it could even begin as a crack beneath your feet! It's all to do with the type of magma bubbling below.

Magma can be thick or runny, depending on the heat, gas and minerals in the rock. The thicker the lava, the more explosive the eruption, as gas bubbles find it harder to escape.

THIN AND RUNNY

Lava flows

Runny magma makes gentler eruptions. These form **shield volcanoes** – the biggest type, with sprawling slopes created by lava flows.

THICK AND STICKY

Cinders

Sticky magma makes explosive eruptions. These form **cinder cone volcanoes,** with steep slopes built up from cinders and ash.

LAYERING

Cinders

Lava flows

Some volcanoes alternate between explosive and gentler eruptions. These form **composite, or stratovolcanoes,** where layers of hardened lava and ash build up into a cone.

PARÍCUTIN

In 1943, a Mexican farmer watched a brand new volcano (Parícutin) being born. It started as a spurt of smoke, ash and rock from a crack that opened up in his corn field!

• A week later, the volcano was a cinder cone over 100m tall. By ten weeks it was three times that height.

• Eruptions continued for nine whole years, until Parícutin went quiet at 424m tall.

MOUNT ST HELENS

Mount St Helens, USA, is a stratovolcano. In 1980, it grew a bulge on one side, which got bigger and bigger until the magma inside it exploded.

• Some 400m blew off the top of the mountain, forming a massive crater.

• Soon afterwards, the volcano began to rebuild itself as small eruptions filled the crater with lava and ash.

CRATERS

Some volcanoes have more than one crater. Mount Etna, in Italy, has four.

LAKES

Some craters contain red-hot lava lakes, where magma has bubbled up to the surface.

CALDERAS

Huge craters, called calderas, form when a magma chamber collapses or explodes.

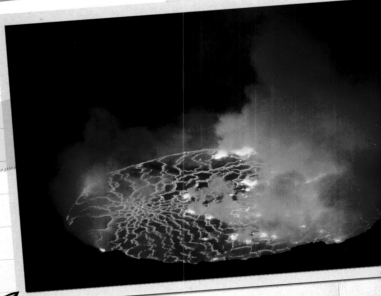

VOLCANO FEATURES

Which volcano made the biggest bang?

Imagine being in England and hearing a sound made in France. It sounds a bit crazy – but not as crazy as the eruption of Krakatau. When this Indonesian volcano exploded in 1883, people heard the blast 4,800km away – nearly 14 times the distance from London to Paris!

Krakatau was an island of about 30 square kilometres, but the eruption blew most of it to dust. About 25 cubic kilometres of rock and ash were blasted into the air – enough to fill 10 MILLION Olympic pools.

The explosion was heard as far away as Australia and the island of Rodrigues,

KRAKATAU'S ASH FELL ON SHIPS AS FAR AS 6,000KM DOWNWIND OF THE ERUPTION.

KRAKATAU

EAR SPLITTING!

Krakatau made the furthest-reaching sound ever recorded in history. Over 160km away, it registered 172 decibels. That's louder than a jet plane at take-off when you're standing right next to it.

According to a ship captain's log book, the bang burst the eardrums of sailors 64km away.

(((((VIBRATIONS))))))

Even when human ears could no longer hear it, weather stations around the world picked up the vibrations. They circled the globe for another five days!

BOOM!

The eruption was 13,000 times more powerful than the Hiroshima atomic bomb of 1945. It darkened the sky for hundreds of kilometres and set off lightning storms.

near Mauritius, where people thought it was the roar of distant gunfire. It triggered tsunamis that wiped out 165 villages and killed tens of thousands of people. Others died from pyroclastic flows that sped across the surface of the ocean.

Anak Krakatau is highly active and grows by about 5m each year.

ASH FROM THE ERUPTION MADE THE MOON LOOK BLUE, OR EVEN GREEN!

MAP OF KRAKATAU, INDONESIA

ANAK KRAKATAU

Outline of island before 26th August 1883

The island today

KRAKATAU ISLAND

REBORN

Krakatau's magma chamber collapsed in the eruption, creating a giant underwater caldera. About 50 years later, a new island appeared there. It's known as Anak Krakatau - Indonesian for 'child of Krakatau'!

Can people tell if an earthquake is coming?

About 100,000 earthquakes are felt by humans every year, and at least 100 of these cause damage. It would help a lot to know when they're coming – but earthquake scientists, called seismologists, are yet to find a successful way of predicting tremors.

On any particular fault line, scientists know there will be an earthquake sometime in the future. The problem is, they can't tell *when* it will happen. There are plenty of theories about warning signs – but as we can't simulate a full-scale earthquake, it's hard to test or prove whether any of them are linked.

PROBABILITY

What seismologists can do is work out the chances of a quake, and how the ground will move, based on a region's history and geology. This helps with planning and making buildings and people safer (see p28).

The US Geological Society releases maps showing the earthquake risk across the USA.

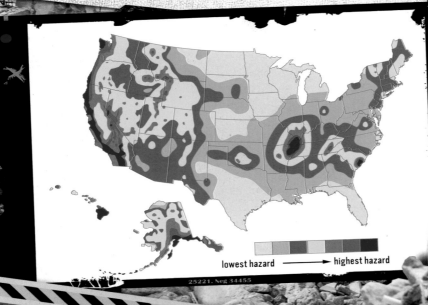

lowest hazard ————→ highest hazard

25221. Neg 34455

>> WARNING <<
ANIMAL INSTINCTS

There have been many reports of animals behaving oddly before earthquakes...

 ELEPHANTS in Thailand ran to high ground hours before the 2004 tsunami.

 HIBERNATING SNAKES in China scooted out of their burrows a month before an earthquake in 1975. This actually saved thousands of lives, as authorities evacuated the area.

 A COLONY OF TOADS abandoned its pond in L'Aquila, Italy in 2009, days before a quake.

 Farmers have noticed their CHICKENS stop laying eggs before large earthquakes. DOGS seem to bark, bite or howl more.

PROBLEM

No one knows for sure what the animals are reacting to.

>> WARNING <<
NATURAL CHANGES

Animals may be more sensitive to these things than humans...

* Electrical changes in the air
* Gases released from Earth
* Changes in magnetic fields
* Chemical changes in groundwater
* Dropping water levels

PROBLEM:

Any of these things can happen without an earthquake following them.

>> WARNING <<
FORESHOCK

This is a smaller earthquake that comes before a big one.

PROBLEM

We can't tell if an earthquake is a foreshock until the larger quake happens.

TSUNAMI
HAZARD ZONE

IN CASE OF EARTHQUAKE. GO TO HIGH GROUND OR INLAND

พื้นที่เสี่ยงภัย
คลื่นยักษ์
เมื่อเกิดแผ่นดินไหวให้หนีห่าง
จากชายหาดและขึ้นที่สูงโดยเร็ว

What harm can an ash cloud do?

When Eyjafjallajökull in Iceland erupted in 2010, it disrupted flights across Europe. But the ash that choked the skies then was just a puff compared to Mount Tambora's! In 1815, this mighty volcano blasted so much debris into the atmosphere that it chilled the world.

Mount Tambora lies on the island of Sumbawa, in modern-day Indonesia. Before the eruption, it was about 4,300m tall – now it's just 2,851m. The volcano ejected about 100 cubic kilometres of ash, rock and gas, firing it over 40km high.

Scalding pyroclastic flows destroyed everyone and everything in their path. Many people who weren't killed instantly died later from disease or starvation. Ash and gas were carried across the world, limiting sunlight and stopping temperatures from rising the following spring and summer.

When Eyjafjallajökull erupted, flights were cancelled because of the risk the ash would damage plane engines.

TAMBORA'S ERUPTION LOWERED GLOBAL TEMPERATURES BY UP TO 3°C!

A YEAR AFER THE ERUPTION...

✱ Monsoon season was disrupted in India.

✱ Devastating floods hit China.

✱ In North America, snow fell in June and frosts continued into July and August. Europe and the USA experienced widespread crop failures and famine.

NO SUMMER ➡ In the northern hemisphere, 1816 became known as 'the year without a summer'!

MONSTER ➡ Many people think the gloom from Tambora inspired Mary Shelley to write *Frankenstein*.

FIERY SUNSETS

When ash particles in the atmosphere scatter the Sun's rays, it can cause extra-fiery sunsets. After Krakatau's eruption in 1883 (see p18), the sunsets were so vivid that fire crews in the USA rushed to put out the 'flames'!

MASTER BLASTERS

100 cubic kilometres of rock and ash

3 — **VESUVIUS AD 79**

TAMBORA 1815

18 — **KRAKATOA 1883**

1 — **MOUNT ST HELENS 1980**

18 — **MOUNT PINATUBO 1991**

RECENT CHILL

In 1991, Mount Pinatubo in the Philippines spewed out about 20 million tonnes of sulphur dioxide. The gas and ash circled the world and cooled the globe by up to 0.5°C over the next two years.

Pinatubo's ash destroyed crops and other plant life.

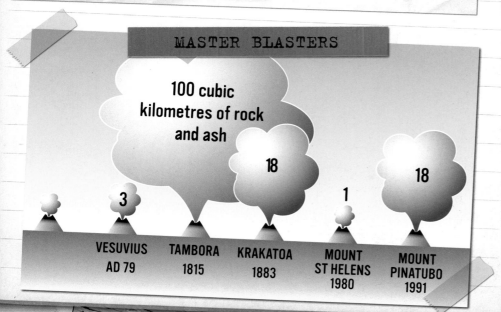

Many villages had to be abandoned after Mount Pinatubo erupted.

Where is a supervolcano waiting to erupt?

Volcano experts are keeping a close eye on Yellowstone National Park, USA. Lurking under the ground there is one of the biggest volcanoes of all time – a supervolcano. This sleeping giant hasn't erupted for 640,000 years, but that doesn't mean it never will again.

The Yellowstone volcano has erupted explosively three times – 2.1 million years ago, 1.3 million years ago and 640,000 years ago. The last eruption left a caldera 80km wide. Scientists believe another eruption could happen, but the chances it will be in our lifetimes are very, very small.

The most recent supervolcano eruption was Mount Toba in Indonesia, 74,000 years ago. It threw out 2,800 cubic kilometres of magma – enough to build more than 19 million Empire State Buildings!

THE LAST LAVA FLOW AT YELLOWSTONE WAS ABOUT 70,000 YEARS AGO.

SUPERVOLCANO

LOOK OUT!

If the Yellowstone supervolcano does ever erupt, more than a trillion tonnes of rock and ash could blast into the atmosphere, smother much of the USA and plunge the world into winter. Yikes!

EVERY YEAR, BETWEEN 1,000 AND 3,000 EARTHQUAKES HAPPEN HERE.

VEI

Scientists measure eruptions on a scale called the Volcanic Explosivity Index (VEI). Mount Tambora (see page 22) had a VEI of 7. A supervolcano scores 8 – that's ten times stronger.

YELLOWSTONE
640,000 years ago
1000 cu km (VEI 8)

LONG VALLEY CALDERA, USA
760,000 years ago
580 cu km (VEI 7)

CRATER LAKE, USA
7,600 years ago
150 cu km (VEI 7)

KRAKATAU 18 cu km (VEI 6)

VESUVIUS 3 cu km (VEI 5)

ST. HELENS 1 cu km (VEI 4)

WEIRD FEATURES

The magma under Yellowstone fuels more than 10,000 geothermal features. These include fountain-like geysers, steaming hot springs and bubbling mud pots.

RAINBOW STEAM

Yellowstone's Grand Prismatic Spring pumps out more than 30 litres of boiling water every second. Its rising steam reflects all the colours of the rainbow!

WATER JET

Old Faithful geyser erupts every 45–90 minutes, spurting superheated water over 50m high.

EGGY MUD

Gurgling mud pots smell like rotten eggs because of a gas called hydrogen sulphide.

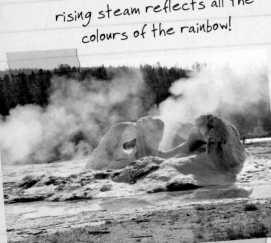

What else is freaky about volcanoes and earthquakes?

LIGHTWEIGHT

The volcanic rock pumice is the only rock that can float on water. It's full of bubbly holes, made by hot gases that burst out of the rock as it cools.

Underwater chimneys, floating rocks, the ground turning to jelly… all these phenomena happen thanks to rumblings in the Earth's plates. Here are a few freaky things you might not know about volcanoes, earthquakes and their fiery forces.

SINKING

During a powerful earthquake, loose, wet soil can act like quicksand. This is called liquefaction. If it happens under streets, it can sink buildings or swallow up cars!

Some volcanoes erupt DIAMONDS in a rare type of magma called kimberlite.

SMOKER

Where plates are moving apart under the ocean, 'black smoker' vents can appear. Water as hot as 400°C jets upwards like a fountain. Amazingly, that doesn't stop tube worms from living there!

DANGER

If you see a lake of water in the crater of a volcano – don't jump in! It could contain enough acid to burn through your skin.

TASTY

At the foot of Mount Unzen in Japan, people boil eggs in magma-heated springs!

KA-BOOM!

You can see lightning in a volcanic ash cloud – it sparks when the particles collide.

What can people do to stay safe?

Testing volcanoes is a red-hot job.

About half a billion people live within 'danger range' of a volcano, and some of the world's largest cities are built right on top of quaking faults. Earthquakes usually happen very suddenly, and volcanoes can explode like a bomb – so how can people avoid disaster?

Eruptions are easier to predict than earthquakes. Volcanologists (volcano scientists) monitor volcanoes for warning signs, such as rising temperatures, leaking gases or lots of small earth tremors. This usually gives them time to alert people and prepare an evacuation.

With earthquakes, seismologists and their equipment are observing plate movements all the time. Some quake-prone countries have systems that raise alarms when they detect the first shock waves. But most help comes in making buildings that can survive a shaking.

A volcanologist approaches an active lava lake in the Democratic Republic of the Congo.

BUILD SAFE

Buildings tend to be safer if the upper floors can sway a bit, but not too much! Builders use steel braces to reinforce walls, as well as special shock-absorbing devices.

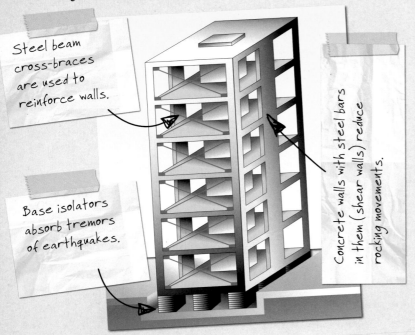

Steel beam cross-braces are used to reinforce walls.

Concrete walls with steel bars in them (shear walls) reduce rocking movements.

Base isolators absorb tremors of earthquakes.

San Francisco's TransAmerica pyramid has a strong but flexible base. It survived a massive quake in 1989.

Taipei 101 in Taiwan is one of the world's tallest skyscrapers. It's made steady by a huge sphere called a damper, near the top, which counteracts the movement of a quake.

EMERGENCY ACTION

When a volcano erupts:

- Evacuate if you're told to and stay out of any restricted zones.

- Avoid river valleys and areas downhill or downwind of the volcano.

- Wear protective clothing, a mask and goggles to avoid harm from ash.

During an earthquake:

- If outside, move away from buildings, trees or power lines and stay down.

- If you're inside, stay there. Take cover under a strong table or desk.

- Stay away from windows and tall furniture that could fall on you.

EARLY WARNINGS

In 2011 (see page 14), Japan's early warning system alerted people in Tokyo a minute before the city shook. The system also halted high-speed trains and factory assembly lines.

Seismic waves whizz so fast, they may only give seconds of warning. But even this can save lives.

Japanese schoolchildren practise an earthquake drill.

What on Earth? words

aftershock A tremor that follows a larger earthquake.

caldera An extra-large crater, formed when a volcano's cone or magma chamber collapses.

cinders Fragments of erupted rock.

core The hot metal mass in the centre of Earth, from 2,900km to 6,378km beneath the surface. The inner core is solid because pressure on it is so intense. The outer core is liquid.

crater The bowl-shaped hollow at the top of a volcano.

crust Earth's surface, made up of continental and oceanic plates. It ranges from 5km to 100km thick.

eruption When a volcano ejects lava, ash and gas through a vent or crack in Earth's crust.

evacuate To remove people from a place of danger.

famine An extreme shortage of food.

fault A fracture in Earth's crust, caused by plate movements.

foreshock A tremor that comes before a larger earthquake.

geology The science of rocks and how Earth is made.

geothermal Relating to or produced by the heat inside Earth.

hot spot A place where extra-hot magma in the mantle rises and burns through a plate.

lahar A destructive mudflow, caused by material from a volcano mixing with large amounts of water.

landslide The collapse of a mass of rock and earth from a mountain, hillside or cliff.

lava Hot molten rock, ejected from a volcano.

lava flow A river of lava pouring down the sides of a volcano.

magma Molten rock beneath Earth's surface.

magma chamber A store of magma within Earth's crust.

magnitude Size or strength. An earthquake is given a number to rate its magnitude.

mantle The layer of stiff molten rock beneath Earth's crust, from 100km to 2,900km deep.

plates The jigsaw-like sections of solid rock that together make up Earth's crust.

pyroclastic flow A fast-moving avalanche of superheated ash, gas and rock from a volcano.

radioactive Giving off radiation, a harmful form of energy produced by nuclear reactions.

reservoir A human-made lake, usually storing water behind a dam.

seismometer An instrument that measures movements in the ground, such as shock waves from an earthquake.

simulate To imitate or accurately recreate something.

spring A place where underground water bubbles to the surface.

sulphur dioxide A toxic gas released by volcanoes.

supervolcano A volcano capable of erupting more than 1,000 cubic kilometres of material.

tsunami A huge, destructive sea wave, triggered by an earthquake, volcano or landslide.

vent The opening from which a volcano erupts.

Further information

BOOKS

Volcanoes (*Our Earth in Action*) by Chris Oxlade, Franklin Watts, 2014

Earthquake Disasters; Tsunami Disasters and *Volcano Disasters* (*Catastrophe* series) by John Hawkins, Franklin Watts, 2014

Tsunami Surges (*Planet in Peril*) by Cath Senker, Wayland, 2015

Volcano & Earthquake (*Eyewitness*) by DK Children, 2014

Earth-Shattering Earthquakes (*Horrible Geography*) by Anita Ganeri and Mike Phillips, Scholastic, 2010

Violent Volcanoes (*Horrible Geography*) by Anita Ganeri and Mike Phillips, Scholastic, 2008

WEBSITES

http://www.volcanodiscovery.com/home.html
A whole range of volcano info, including photos and maps.

http://education.nationalgeographic.co.uk/education/encyclopedia/volcano/?ar_a=1
Volcano info and photos from the National Geographic.

http://www.bbc.co.uk/programmes/articles/14zZfpg3vmb9r4FB9mCHjy/live-volcano-webcams
Check out the latest volcano activity through live webcams.

http://news.bbc.co.uk/cbbcnews/hi/find_out/guides/tech/volcanoes/newsid_1768000/1768595.stm
Facts about volcanoes from the BBC Newsround programme.

http://earthquake.usgs.gov/earthquakes/
Site of the USGS Earthquake Hazards Program. You can find the Volcano Hazards Program here:
https://volcanoes.usgs.gov

http://www.nps.gov/yell/index.htm
Explore Yellowstone National Park.

CLIPS

http://www.bbc.co.uk/science/earth/surface_and_interior/plate_boundary
http://www.bbc.co.uk/science/earth/natural_disasters/volcano
Various clips from the BBC.

http://video.nationalgeographic.com/video/volcano-eruptions
A mash-up of eruptions and lava flows – watch a truck trying to escape.

https://www.youtube.com/watch?v=dAUILQIj_wk
See Yellowstone's geysers in action.

http://www.bbc.co.uk/science/earth/natural_disasters/supervolcano#p00gfjpg
Discover the supervolcano lurking under the USA.

https://www.youtube.com/watch?v=CtBXTvtFaCU
Find out what happens when an earthquake strikes.